The F&I Revolution
Finance - Reimagined

Michael A. Bennett

ISBN-10: 1507777221
ISBN-13: 978-1507777220

HERE'S WHAT OTHERS SAY ABOUT MIKE BENNETT AND THE TWO MINUTE PRESENTATION

Mike Bennett trained me in the early 1990's right out of sales and I have spent the last 20 years as an F&I producer. Last year I finished the year at over $2200 per copy and over 70% service contract penetration. I've worked with many people over the years and have seen several selling methods. I'm convinced that Mike's "Two Minute Presentation" revolutionized the industry and is unmatched.

Johnny Miramon
Finance Director Galpin Ford

I've never seen anyone in the business that could find way to go in a car deal better than Mike Bennett. He is the finest Finance man I know.

Mike Dennis General Manager

In 3 generations of business we have never allowed a trainer or consultant in our dealership. Mike is the exception to the rule. I've always said, "if they were any good they would be in a dealership still being that good." Mike Bennett is really that good!

Archie Solomon
Owner/Dealer principal
Solomon Chevrolet Cadillac

I worked for Mike nearly a decade as his Finance Director. We had as many as thirteen producers at one time and the system Mike Bennett trains is the best in the business.

Wade Folmer

I was selling cars for many years. Mike Bennett is the only training I've been exposed to and I run $1500 per copy consistently and have done that from day one of my Finance career.

John Carter Finance Manager
New South Ford Nissan

Mike can train anyone. He has trained beginners and immediately taken them to high numbers and has taken the old timers that we couldn't get to accept change and turned them around with his process. I've never seen anyone work with such a diverse bunch of personalities with so much success.

Ty Townsend
Townsed Automotive Group

I was only producing $550 per copy when Mike started training at our dealership and have reached numbers as high as $1600 per unit and held them. Mikes "Two Minute System" is the best I've ever seen.

Jamal Likkle F&I producer

I've had many trainers help me with finance training over the last twenty years and Mike Bennett's "Two Minute Presentation" produces the absolutely best results I've ever seen. That's why I've partnered with him for our on-line training at Paul Webb VT. Our on-line training is available for any dealer. Mike Bennett is our Finance training partner.

Paul Webb Owner
Paul Webb Training

I have come to depend on Mike Bennett for all of my F&I development. He has produced the results that nobody else could. He has trained for me for years. He has helped my newcomers and my old-timers. He is the best.

Bob Aubrey
General Manager Patty Peck Honda

When I started training for Mike I thought I was good, (and I was) but Mike helped me become great. The "Two Minute Presentation" is better than anything I've ever seen and seen everything!

Dana Gaudet Lead Trainer
Mike Bennett and Associates F&I Development

I've seen Mike train his system on Docupad, Itap and many other platforms with great success. His process works in every market, with every platform and with every producer. I've never seen anything like it. He is the best in the industry.

Bob McKinney Agency Principal
Paragon Dealer Services

Michael A. Bennett

Disclaimer: No part of this publication may be reproduced or transmitted in any form or by any means, mechanical or electronic, including photocopying or recording, or by any information storage and retrieval system, or transmitted by email without permission in writing from the publisher. While all attempts have been made to verify the information provided in this book, neither the author nor the publisher assumes any responsibility for errors, omissions, or contrary interpretations of the subject matter herein. The views expressed are those of the author alone, and should not be taken as expert instruction or commands. The reader is responsible for his or her own actions. Adherence to all applicable laws and regulations, including international, federal, state and local governing professional licensing, business practices , advertising , and all other aspects of doing business in the United States, or any other country jurisdiction is the sole responsibility of the purchaser or reader. Neither the author nor the publisher assume any responsibility or liability whatsoever on the behalf of the purchaser or reader of these materials. Any perceived slight to any individual or organization purely unintentional. Please consider leaving a review wherever you bought the book or telling your friends about it. Help spread the word. Thank you for purchasing and reading my book. I would love to hear your comments and thoughts on "The F&I Revolution – Finance Reimagined" and find out if it has helped you grow your business.

CONTENTS

INTRODUCTION

There are many training ideas in our industry for F & I sales. Unfortunately, there are few that give an easy to follow MAP for selling. It is important to understand the law and industry ethics, but knowledge of these things will not help you sell products.

I decided to share this MAP with other finance people to help them do their job easier, faster and more effectively.

I was a car salesman for nearly five years when an opportunity to apply for a finance producer's job came up and I campaigned for the position like a politician. After several weeks I was finally given the chance.

There were two finance producers in our dealership that had turned in their resignation within a couple of weeks of each other. This gave me the perfect opportunity.

Immediately after I started, one man left abruptly and the other had a family medical emergency and left within two days.

What about training?

Luckily, I had a sales manager who had done some finance. He was excellent at administrative paperwork, but a poor product salesman.

Within a few weeks I became very efficient at getting all the paperwork signed. I figured out how to streamline the paperwork process out of necessity. Our store was selling around one hundred and eighty-five cars per month, and for the first few months I was the only finance person.

The store did hire a finance director to be my supervisor, but it took four months to find him and get him started.

I thought that having an experienced finance director would help me learn to sell, but it didn't. This director was great at legal and ethical processes, but not much of a product salesperson. I was still on my own.

It took a couple of months to learn the paperwork, interacting with banks and getting control of the administrative part of the job.

Once that was under control I began to try my hand at selling.

Our store was not big on outside training, so I started experimenting with how to sell service contracts.

I took an extended service contract brochure home and asked my wife to listen to me 'pitch' this product and give me her opinion. We did this for several nights until she couldn't stand to see me come home, and I had to stop.

I did develop a basic design for selling service contracts during these first few nights. From there, I challenged myself to get better.

I produced finance for this dealership for several years. During this time our store grew to over two hundred units per month. I produced an average of one hundred and twenty deals per month and the director covered the rest.

Later I was promoted to a position over finance. We grew to

average over 500 units every month. Our store had a director and five full time producers. Our average was well over $1200 per unit.

Our top producer maintained an $1800 per unit average, and we had many producers at all levels in between.

We counted all sales, even high mileage units, employee purchase units, cheap wholesale to the public units and all subprime.

During the time I was a producer and, throughout nearly ten thousand car deals, as you will read, I learned to sell many products and developed this system that allowed all of these products to be effectively presented in two minutes.

This presentation is still being used in that dealership and by hundreds of producers in stores all over the nation in domestic, import, high line, luxury specialty, power sports, RV, motorcycle and in metro and rural markets.

This process has revolutionized the industry.

Including the administrative paperwork and my product presentation I could get customers in and out of my office in an average of twenty minutes while still maintaining this level of 'dollars per copy'.

We have this training program available on line and with in-store trainers across the nation. Enjoy this book, and remember, those of you working in dealerships as producers today are the industry leaders of tomorrow.

Lead with skill!

To learn more about our in store and online training programs please go to www.bennetttraining.com

1

IT STARTS WITH SALES

Selling in F & I starts with your salespeople. Many of us sold vehicles before entering finance. We all have similar experiences in how we were treated by the 'F & I GURU'.

Some finance managers experience memory loss when they enter this position. They forget what it was like to be a salesperson. Salespeople work hard to sell a vehicle, and it's important to remember this when interacting with them.

It's not always as simple as taking an order and doing the paperwork.

Your salesperson may have spent hours, days, or even weeks trying to convince someone to buy.

When a finance manager is short or not supportive about a deal, they lose credibility with their team, and the salespeople are YOUR team.

For a finance manager to succeed, they need as many deals as possible in front of them each month. It helps if these deals are complete, with all the paperwork in order. Take care of your team and you'll have a better chance of getting their cooperation.

Attitude is as important to your success as ability. If you keep a positive attitude about the car deals your salespeople bring you, they will keep a positive attitude about bringing you car deals.

In a large store environment where there are several finance producers, getting your share of opportunities is vital. You can't sell products if you don't get opportunities. Time is very important to everyone.

It's important to your managers. If they get busy and have several deals backed up they won't want to wait while you spend an hour or more with each customer.

Your sales manager would be elated if you could 'spin' your deals in twenty minutes. (Spin is a fond term for processing a deal.) A happy sales manager is a supportive sales manager.

As a finance person, you will need all the support you can get from management.

If you take too long with each deal, your customers will become very impatient. Nobody in the dealership wants to deal with impatient customers while they wait for finance.

Your salespeople will be more cooperative if you can get to their people quickly and get them signed up. The car deal isn't done until they come out of finance.

Above all, your customer is conscious of time. Statistically, the most undesirable part of buying a vehicle is, "It takes too long."

Solve this problem and you will gain the respect of your managers, salespeople, and most importantly, your customer.

Sometimes delays will happen that are unavoidable, but we should always focus on normal car sales.

It's so easy to fool ourselves into believing that spinning our deals in twenty minutes and still maintaining a high average dollar amount is not possible, but it really is.

2

PREPARE YOUR DEAL

When a vehicle is sold, the salesperson will bring the deal jacket into finance.

It's very important to have a good enough relationship with your salespeople to expect their paperwork to be correct.

If your paperwork is half filled out, there is no mileage, the serial number is not readable, or the name or address on the worksheet is wrong, it will be impossible to accomplish a Twenty Minute Spin. If this problem exists, nobody can correct it but the finance manager.

You may want to be demanding and maybe even aggressive in how you handle this problem, but before you result to this kind of behavior, first try to explain the benefit of good paperwork and how it helps with time management in processing their deal. If they will listen, try to reason with your people.

Remember that they are your team, and you need them to feed your business.

If all else fails, result to whatever means necessary to correct the problem. You can't succeed without excellent paperwork.

Have your salesperson sit with you while you go through the deal jacket and load all your information into the computer. If you allow them to leave for any reason and you find missing information, you have to try to locate them and wait. Now you are STOPPED until the salesperson returns to correct the problem.

DO NOT LET THIS HAPPEN TO YOU, EVER!!!

Once you have all of your information in the computer, let your salesperson leave while you print your preliminary administrative paperwork and prepare your product presentation.

Your preliminary administrative paperwork will consist of the title paperwork (trade and sold vehicles), privacy notice, any state or dealer required disclosures, insurance forms and everything else that does not have to do with product and financing.

Save all of your financing and product paperwork for after your sales presentation. After your paperwork is printed, set up your menu.

Remember, your primary responsibility as a finance manager is to sell finance products.

Setting up your menu correctly and quickly is a must.

Most producers lose the majority of their time right here. They are not organized in how they acquire the product costs.

I RECOMMEND TWO DIFFERENT FOUR COLUMN MENU OPTIONS.

MENU ONE

1.   Column one

All products at 66 month payment

2.   Column two

Remove one product at 66 months

3.   Column three

Remove another product at 66 months

4.   Column four

Replace all products at 72 months

MENU EXAMLE:

Vision Auto Enterprises	Repayment Options		Deal, Test Silvertone 2008 Chevrolet Equinox

Sale Price: $11,156.40   Sales Tax: $55.78   Trade Allowance: $200.00   Payoff: $0.00   Doc Fee: $489.50   License / Registration Fees and Taxes: $16.50

Platinum	Gold	Silver	Bronze
Extended Service Plan	**Extended Service Plan**	**Extended Service Plan**	**Extended Service Plan**
· Pays 100% of covered Labor and Parts. Includes Towing, Rental and Roadside Assistance · Comprehensive mechanical & electrical breakdown coverage	· Pays 100% of covered Labor and Parts. Includes Towing, Rental and Roadside Assistance · Comprehensive mechanical & electrical breakdown coverage	· Pays 100% of covered Labor and Parts. Includes Towing, Rental and Roadside Assistance · Comprehensive mechanical & electrical breakdown coverage	· Pays 100% of covered Labor and Parts. Includes Towing, Rental and Roadside Assistance · Comprehensive mechanical & electrical breakdown coverage
GAP Protection	**GAP Protection**	**GAP Protection**	**GAP Protection**
· GAP Protection Picks Up Where the Insurance Company Leaves Off. · In The Event Of A Total Loss, Gap Pays The Difference Between The Loan Payoff And What Your Insurance Deems Replacement Value, Also Covers Your Deductible Up To $1000.	· GAP Protection Picks Up Where the Insurance Company Leaves Off. · In The Event Of A Total Loss, Gap Pays The Difference Between The Loan Payoff And What Your Insurance Deems Replacement Value, Also Covers Your Deductible Up To $1000.	· GAP Protection Picks Up Where the Insurance Company Leaves Off. · In The Event Of A Total Loss, Gap Pays The Difference Between The Loan Payoff And What Your Insurance Deems Replacement Value, Also Covers Your Deductible Up To $1000.	· GAP Protection Picks Up Where the Insurance Company Leaves Off. · In The Event Of A Total Loss, Gap Pays The Difference Between The Loan Payoff And What Your Insurance Deems Replacement Value, Also Covers Your Deductible Up To $1000.
Tire & Wheel	**Tire & Wheel**		**Tire & Wheel**
· Protection from all road hazards · Repair or replace all tires and wheels and charges associated with the repair or replacement.	· Protection from all road hazards · Repair or replace all tires and wheels and charges associated with the repair or replacement.		· Protection from all road hazards · Repair or replace all tires and wheels and charges associated with the repair or replacement.
Credit Life			**Credit Life**
· Provides a free and clear title to the beneficiary in the event of death			· Provides a free and clear title to the beneficiary in the event of death
Term: 66 Payment: $282.73	Term: 66 Payment: $276.49	Term: 66 Payment: $270.10	Term: 72 Payment: $263.45

I understand this is not a contract or offer to purchase. It is a description of the optional products that are available to purchase and the estimated monthly payment for each choice. I understand I must qualify to obtain financing and the payment may vary based on my credit. The base payment on 66 months is $204.51 on an interest rate of 6.04. The base payment on 72 months is $190.15 on an interest rate of 6.04. The finance charges, amount financed, total of payments, and total of payments including the down payment will be disclosed on my actual finance contract. The dealer makes no warranties, whether expressed or implied.

X _____   X _____   X _____
Purchaser's Signature   Co-purchaser's Signature   Date

Wednesday, January 29, 2014 8:17 AM

Let's talk about the philosophy of this setup.

Obviously, the last column will have all the products and the lowest payment option for the customer because of the extended term. By setting the menu up in this format we have the ability to begin desensitizing our customer to a higher payment.

This is not a new idea. Salespeople have been doing this forever. I learned it when I was selling cars.

It's the old "stick'em to the ceiling, then peel'em off" philosophy.

The traditional menu will have:

1.   All products in column one at 72 months

2. One less product in column two at 72 months

3. One less product in column three at 72 months

4. One or two products maximum in column four at 72 months

Why is this idea bad?

Over the nearly ten thousand deals I did while creating this process, I conducted several studies.

I based one of the studies on how many people would buy the first time they were asked. The results were very interesting. I will use one hundred deals to make this example.

Out of 100 deals, there are 60 potential sales. One or more products will be sold when we achieve the skill level this process teaches.

100 Deals

1. 20 will buy everything in the column with the lowest payment, regardless of how many products are there, the first time we ask for the sale

2. 20 will buy a percentage of products in the column with the lowest payment after minimal effort to overcome objections and close

3. The other 20 will only buy if we are skilled enough to change their mind through skilled objection handling

I've always claimed the difference between a good salesperson and a great salesperson is

THE ABILITY TO CHANGE SOMEONE'S MIND

Based on this evidence, why would you ever offer a menu that didn't have every product in the column with the lowest payment? Most finance trainers or training companies struggle with low income producers ($500 to $600 per copy).

Helping a producer move their numbers from the $500 - $600 range to $800 - $1000 is generally as simple as installing this process.

By understanding the buying habits of people and their unwillingness to deal with conflict, coupled with a great process for delivering the value and asking for the sale, it becomes easier to help people improve their production.

The only requirement is consistency in the process.

Moving the $1000 and up producers requires much more training in closing techniques, which we will discuss later in this book.

MENU TWO

1. All products for 36 months

2. All products for 48 months

3. All products for 60 months

4. All products for 72 months

MENU EXAMPLE:

MoConnell Automotive   Repayment Options   RUSTAND, WHITNEY
2014 GMC TERRAIN

Sale Price: $26,233.26   Sales Tax: $961.08   Rebate: $600.00   Trade Allowance: $6,000.00   Payoff: $4,930.73   Doc Fee: $499.50
License / Registration Fees and Taxes: $33.00

Preferred Plus	Preferred	Standard	Economy
CNA Vehicle Service Contract	**CNA Vehicle Service Contract**	**CNA Vehicle Service Contract**	**CNA Vehicle Service Contract**
· Pays 100% of covered Labor and Parts less deductible · Towing and Rental Allowance	· Pays 100% of covered Labor and Parts less deductible · Towing and Rental Allowance	· Pays 100% of covered Labor and Parts less deductible · Towing and Rental Allowance	· Pays 100% of covered Labor and Parts less deductible · Towing and Rental Allowance
Guaranteed Asset Protection	**Guaranteed Asset Protection**	**Guaranteed Asset Protection**	**Guaranteed Asset Protection**
· Picks up where the insurance company leaves off · In the event your vehicle is totaled or stolen and unrecovered, GAP pays the difference of your payoff and the insurance	· Picks up where the insurance company leaves off · In the event your vehicle is totaled or stolen and unrecovered, GAP pays the difference of your payoff and the insurance	· Picks up where the insurance company leaves off · In the event your vehicle is totaled or stolen and unrecovered, GAP pays the difference of your payoff and the insurance	· Picks up where the insurance company leaves off · In the event your vehicle is totaled or stolen and unrecovered, GAP pays the difference of your payoff and the insurance
Tire & Wheel	**Tire & Wheel**	**Tire & Wheel**	**Tire & Wheel**
· Protection from all road hazards · Repair or replace all tires and wheels	· Protection from all road hazards · Repair or replace all tires and wheels	· Protection from all road hazards · Repair or replace all tires and wheels	· Protection from all road hazards · Repair or replace all tires and wheels
Key Replacement	**Key Replacement**	**Key Replacement**	**Key Replacement**
· Replaces the key if lost, stolen, or destroyed.	· Replaces the key if lost, stolen, or destroyed.	· Replaces the key if lost, stolen, or destroyed.	· Replaces the key if lost, stolen, or destroyed.
Term: 36 Payment: $841.57	Term: 48 Payment: $639.27	Term: 60 Payment: $547.94	Term: 72 Payment: $437.10

I understand this is not a contract or offer to purchase. It is a description of the optional products that are available to purchase and the estimated monthly payment for each choice. I understand I must qualify to obtain financing and the payment may vary based on my credit. The base payment on 36 months is $757.48 on an interest rate of 2.59. The base payment on 48 months is $575.39 on an interest rate of 2.59. The base payment on 60 months is $466.19 on an interest rate of 2.59. The base payment on 72 months is $393.43 on an interest rate of 2.59. The finance charges, amount financed, total of payments, and total of payments including the down payment will be disclosed on my actual finance contract. The dealer makes no warranties, whether expressed or implied.

x_____   x_____   x_____
Purchaser's Signature   Co-purchaser's Signature   Date

Monday, March 03, 2014 8:57 PM

The four term menu accomplishes the same results. Your customer will never have an option that doesn't include every product.

This menu is more aggressive, but the producers who use this one always run better numbers. These are the two preferred menu formats of this course.

I've seen many menu formats over my career that have had some success, but sometimes the success happens in spite of the process due to an extremely great closer.

These great closers always improve when they move to this system.

Obviously, if you have an automated menu system, you will be able to calculate or build your menu in an efficient manner.
There are so many different automated and fully integrated systems available on the market today that very few people will need to manually create a menu of payments.

If you do need to create a menu manually, you can have a template that only requires the payment section be filled in at the bottom. Assume you will close every product every time.

What do you pitch if you have a cash customer? It's simple, pitch everything. What a great way to establish whether or not you have a real cash customer. By pitching everything, you will position yourself for a cash conversion or to steal the loan from a credit union or conventional bank

Later, when we go over presenting this pitch to our customer (s), there will be an example of how to accomplish the cash conversion process.

You should have spent only a few minutes preparing the menu for your presentation. Now you're ready to 'take' your T.O.

Stack all of your paperwork on your desk in the order it is to be signed with your menu at the bottom turned over so it appears to be a blank piece of paper.

When you get the administrative paperwork complete you will be at the menu. Now you're ready to transition into your presentation.

3

LEARN TO READ YOUR CUSTOMER

Now, before we go into the showroom to introduce ourselves to the customer(s), we should be aware that not all people process information in the same manner. Some people need to be shown, others need to have things explained and others need to be made comfortable, or to feel good about things. There are also those who process information in some combination of the three.

These are the basic methods in which people process information and by which you can either make a connection or fail to make a connection.

How do you process information?

The problem with sales for most of us is that we tend to sell the way that we process, and only a percentage of our customers will process the same way that we sell.

Most great sales people instinctively adapt their selling technique to match the buying method of their customer.
This has been referred to as 'Unconscious competence.'

The goal of this explanation is to help those of us who do not possess this instinctive ability to learn to do this on purpose.
How do you do that?

It can take years of education and training to become an expert at techniques like this. This book is in no way trying to convince anyone that they can develop these skills through this simple explanation.

However, there are a few basic things that you can watch for that may give you an indication of how your customer might process information.

For example:

A visual processor will tend to look up when asked a question that requires thought or consideration prior to answering.

- A visual processor will tend to use language that is visual like,

- "I see what you mean,"

Or

- "I like the way this looks."

An auditory processor will tend to look side to side when thinking about an answer and use auditory language like,

- "I hear what you're saying,"

Or

- "I like the sound of that."

An emotional processor will tend to look down and use language like,

- "I like the way this feels,"

Or

- "I'm comfortable with that."

Again, this is only a small example of different ways that people may process information.

It is my experience that the more a salesperson learns about basic human behavior, the better salesperson they become.

4

THE PERFECT T.O. FROM SALES

There are many methods throughout the industry for getting the perfect T.O. (turn over) from salespeople.

It's almost impossible to get a group of salespeople to consistently T.O. their customers to finance. Some will not care, some will try to blend their own ideas into the turn, and some are just not capable of handling the transition smoothly.

After several years of struggling with this problem, I surrendered to the idea that no 'group' of salespeople would ever satisfy my need for a great, controlled T.O. So I decided to handle it myself. I accidentally stumbled into a technique that has proven to be the most effective tool in quickly gaining control of a customer.

Although I had very little training, I did receive some T.O. training once. It was terrible. They told me to teach my salespeople to help me slow my customers down. I was instructed to stop my customer half way to my office and tell them, "Before we get to my office, can I get you something to drink? This is going to take a while."

How can a customer have a great attitude with a T.O. like that?

When I tried this technique, every customer I said this to immediately became discouraged and agitated.

Now I was taking a customer with a normal attitude about the finance office and making them hate me. This was unacceptable to me, so I disregarded that training immediately!

I realized that I'd created a reaction from the customer opposite of the one I wanted.

Out of frustration, I walked out one day to the salesman's desk where he and his customers were waiting.

I decided to experiment with some different techniques to try to put the customer in a better mood before bringing them into my office.

It took several attempts before I stumbled onto the right plan. It went like this:

The salesman was in the middle of a sentence when I walked up and politely interrupted him and introduced myself.

FINANCE MANAGER

"Hello, my name is_____, and I'm going to take care of your state and federal paperwork. Come with me and I'll have you out of here in just a few minutes."

A couple of things happened.

The customer seemed to be very excited when I said they would be finished quickly. The salesman stopped talking and didn't have to participate in the T.O. (It's hard to say the wrong thing when you don't say anything)

I acquired complete control of the customers without even trying, and they had a great attitude!

After realizing what had just happened, I decided to perfect this technique and make it part of my routine.

I began to train salespeople to set me up by just visiting with their customers until I was ready, and then stop talking when I walked up.

I had come up with the perfect, 'trainable' T.O.

After I started to my office with the customer in tow, it was time to try my new method of rapport building.

I knew that, if I could get them to like me before we got to my office, I would have a much better chance of getting them to willingly listen to my value building presentation.

Half way to my office I stopped, looked them right in the eye and said,

"Now listen, when we get to my office, don't get comfortable. I'm going to have you out of my office so fast that your seat won't get warm! This is going to be the best experience that you've ever had in a dealership. I promise."

I produced finance for several years after this realization and never again struggled with a good transition from sales to finance.

The customers always followed me to my office with a terrific attitude. This made the chance of selling something much greater.

Also, I learned something about getting control of customers, and what helps make them feel better about the car buying experience.

Speed!

The average customer has the perception that buying a vehicle takes much longer than it should. (In most stores, this is true)

So, starting from the initial greeting try to reinforce how fast and easy this is going to be.

If your customer starts out feeling good about how things are going, they are more apt to continue having a good attitude about being with you.

A good attitude equals a better chance of them saying "Yes" when you ask them to buy something. Another thing I learned was to get the customer involved and busy right from the beginning.

Telling them to "Come with me" was a directive. If you handle this politely and professionally, your customer enters into the relationship taking directions.

If you have a plan, and can explain it to your customer in such a way they understand it and have confidence in you, they will follow you like a puppy. If you continue with this same tactic throughout the entire presentation, you increase your chances when you get to the product presentation.

5

THE PRE-CUSTOMER INTERVIEW

The traditional method of F&I selling suggests that a producer should always interview the customer before bringing them into the finance office. The goal is to uncover information that will allow us to;

1. Set up the term and mileage of our service contract so it is customized to our customer's driving habits and ownership cycle

2. Gather information that we can use against them in our closing arguments

3. Find common ground and build rapport

The only problem with this process is it doesn't work well. It is very difficult to train a finance producer to effectively and consistently use this method.

1. When deals get backed up, it's the first step that gets skipped. Anything that cannot be done 100% of the time should be eliminated from the process

2. It almost always raises suspicion in the customer

3. It takes unnecessary time

Let's address the first of these three concerns:

I used to think that the high volume environment that I was thrown into when I started learning to do finance was so much different than most finance producers, (nearly 200 deals per month), and in some areas that is true.

However, when it comes to the interview process, nearly all producers find themselves in the same position with volume. Most producers are not handling 200 deals per month, but the deals they handle seem to come in bunches, so the effect is the same.

A well trained producer will do the interview process consistently until they get backed up with several deals at once, and they will skip this step to save time.

When we skip steps, the process begins to break down. We get out of our routine and we lose control of our process.

Okay, now let's look at the second issue: It almost always raises suspicion.

If our plan creates suspicion or distrust with the customer prior to bringing them into our office, we have already created an obstacle that needs a solution.

Let's eliminate the obstacle.

So let's look at what we are trying to accomplish in this 'interview' part of the traditional method.
1.   How many miles do you drive per year?

2.   How long do you plan to own the vehicle?

3.   Will anyone else be driving the vehicle?

4.   Where do you plan to garage the vehicle?

I have proven that it is unnecessary to customize the service contract to the customer's driving habits.

Build the term and mileage consistently every time. I prefer a 6 year/100,000 mile plan with a zero deductible.

The only time I will vary from this is when the loan is pre-extended to a longer term, or if I have somehow learned that the customer drives unusually high miles.

The salesperson may have learned this information during his sales process and shared it with me.

When I get to the second stage of overcoming objections restructure service contract, you will learn more about this in a later chapter, I have found it very easy to simply ask,

"How many miles do you drive per year?"

Doing this at the appropriate time eliminates the possibility of creating unnecessary suspicion.

The third problem:

It takes too much time

This one is the most important of all. The faster we get our deal ready and get the customer into our office to begin signing the better our chances become of selling them the product.
An unhappy customer is far less likely to be open minded and listen to a value building presentation.

It generally takes too long to get through the purchase process for most customers. By the time the deal gets to finance, the customer is ready to leave.

We can try to slow them down (creating discomfort and irritability) or we can be efficient and get them in faster than they expected, and create relief and a positive experience.

1. When our customer is happy, they like us.

2. When they like us, they are more willing to listen.

3. When they are listening, they hear, see or feel the value.

4. When this happens they will buy.

Now, if you're a producer who is changing from a pre-customer interview system and would still like to have this information prior to closing, there is a simple way to accomplish this during the administrative paperwork stage.

While signing the title application ask,

"Will anyone else be driving the vehicle?"

This is a place to ask the question that will not raise suspicion. If they ask,

"Why do you need that information?"

You simply explain that

"If someone else is going to be driving the vehicle, this is where we would put them on the title."

We both know that we don't want to add anyone to the title. If the other driver is too young it's easy to explain why they can't be on the title, and anyone else can be explained away by telling them that they would have to be added to the loan.

Remember, we are only trying to find out if a teenager or young college student or someone like that is going to be driving so we can establish a greater need for a service contract or GAP protection.

Young people are hard on mechanical things, increasing the need for added protection, and they tend to drive and park around other young and less responsible people, increasing the need for GAP.

I have found that the need to explain why you're asking the questions very rarely arises. When we ask the right question at the correct place, it does not create suspicion.

During the trade odometer signing, ask,

"Did you buy this vehicle new?"

You can do the math for the average annual miles driven in your head.

If they say no,

"No, I didn't buy it new."

Simply ask;

"How many miles were on the vehicle when you bought it?"

When they are signing the odometer statement for the new vehicle they are buying, you can comment on how nice the vehicle is and ask,

"How long do you plan to own this vehicle?"

I have found it unnecessary to gather this information early, but it is so easy to get it, if you want to, without creating objections or suspicion.

6

GET YOUR CUSTOMER INVOLVED

We started getting the customer involved by our self-controlled T.O.

Now let's get to work on setting up our sales presentation. Although we are primarily finance product 'salespeople', the administrative paperwork must be signed by finance people.

And let's be honest, if we were not required to sell anything, the dealership could easily hire someone for a small hourly wage to do paperwork. They could even train someone to call deals into banks and negotiate with the buyers.

Great F&I people are great salespeople.

Without the great sales numbers we would just be overpaid clerks.

Due to the dynamic of a car dealership, there is no other way to efficiently accomplish this, without using the F&I producer. Let's use this to our advantage.

When your customer follows you into your office, be prepared. Have all of your preliminary paperwork ready to sign, and have your desk and office clear of anything that may be distracting. In sales we are trained to keep things on our desk as a distraction for customers while we are getting a trade appraised or at the desk getting numbers. I agree with this for salespeople, but finance is different. You are with your customers the entire time and need NO distractions.

Anything that distracts them could keep their attention off of your presentation.

A well set up finance office should resemble a physician's waiting area.

It should be clean and comfortable, even a little elegant, but not distracting. I have heard great F&I people state that they wish they could have deep, soft carpet as well, that way their customers would walk in and immediately feel like the office is more inviting.

Personally, I think that is a fantastic idea.

Having a very nice finance office helps in other areas of the sale as well. In most cases, it's the last place the customer will be, and that is how they will remember the store. Let's have them leave with a great last impression.

CSI is very important to us, generally because the managers put pressure on us to keep it high or our pay plans are attached to it. Shouldn't it be important to us anyway? I think it should 'absolutely' be one of the most important things we concern ourselves with.

Career finance experts will always agree that a happy customer will return to the dealership and will want to deal with the same people who treated them well.

Suppose you don't sell all of your products to someone but they have a great experience, the chance of selling them more the next time and making more profit as they begin to trust you will increase with every purchase, the same as sales.

Before the customer(s) sits down, give them a pen and have them start signing something. Don't rush them, but keep the flow of paperwork moving.

This accomplishes three things.

1. It gets the paperwork out of the way

2. It reinforces the fact that this will only take a few minutes

3. It gets them involved

When the customer sees the stack of paperwork quickly disappearing, they start to believe this really is going to be over quickly. The customer continues to develop a positive attitude.

Develop a descriptive explanation of every form you give them that will answer any question they may come up with before they ask.

If you can anticipate a question and answer it in the explanation, you will keep control.

When they don't understand something and have to stop your presentation to ask, control is lost. With every 'spin', you will develop a better explanation of each form until you accomplish a polished presentation.

Keeping the flow of your presentation moving smoothly will help you maintain control and stay on task. Knowing what you are going to do next will help you develop the skill to be sidetracked by your customer and go right back to your process without getting lost. Remember that every move helps you set up the next one.

You should build confidence with every step.

When you get to the office with your customer it is very important to disclose price and payment before starting the paperwork. When you begin the administrative paperwork without pro-actively going over their payment disclosure you can create an environment of distrust. Once you have created this environment it is very difficult to correct.

Imagine that you have just sat down with your customers and started the administrative signing and your customer says,

"Before we sign anything I'd like to see the numbers"

If you allow this situation to occur you have created questionable situation that your customer was afraid of and now they may not recover.

Most finance training methods encourage the producer to disclose the base payment at the menu presentation.

I prefer to separate the two events. When the customer sits down I say,

"Before we start the paperwork I would like to go over your price and payments to make sure that everything is the way you agreed, is that okay?"

I guarantee a positive response from the customer every time, plus you gain their confidence because they no longer have to worry about any deception from you so they will be more receptive as you go through the process.

"Now that we have that out of the way, let's start with the_____ form"

Now we can begin the administrative paperwork.

When addressing your customer(s), you need to decide, case by case, how to address them. Some will respond well to Mr. / Mrs. and some will allow a more intimate interaction. Use the more intimate path whenever it's appropriate.

For the sake of this demonstration we will use a more formal example.

GOOD EXAMPLE:

FINANCE PERSON

"Mr. _____, this is a title application so we can get the title to your new vehicle registered in your name."

CUSTOMER

"Okay."

BAD EXAMPLE:

FINANCE PERSON

"Mr. _____, this is a title application."

CUSTOMER

"What is this for?"

FINANCE PERSON

"It's so we can get the vehicle registered in your name."

See the difference?

The first way you keep everything moving forward and the second way the customer interrupts the process.

GOOD EXAMPLE:

FINANCE PERSON

"This is a privacy notice. It explains the rights that you have to keep our dealership from giving out your private information to others."

CUSTOMER

"Great!"

BAD EXAMPLE:

FINANCE PERSON

"Sign this privacy notice."

CUSTOMER

"What is this for?"

FINANCE PERSON

"This form says that your privacy is protected."

Again, see the difference?

You're going to answer these questions either way, so you might as well control the flow of your presentation as you do.

If your customer constantly has to ask questions or clarify each piece of paper, it will put them in a defensive position. A customer in a defensive position is less likely to develop a trust in you.

Without a trust in you they are less likely to buy. You will complete the signing of the administrative paperwork much more quickly with this process.

Saving time in administrative areas is very important; closing may take some extra time. Save up as much time as you can by streamlining the things in your 'spin', that don't have anything to do with selling.

EXAMPLE:

FINANCE PERSON

"Mr. _____, this is an odometer statement explaining how many miles are on the vehicle you are purchasing. Sign right here.
"Mrs. _____, while he is signing the odometer statement, this is the title application. With this form we can get the title for the new vehicle in your name.

"Mr.   , while Mrs._   is signing the title application, you can sign the proof of insurance form.
This form says that you agree to keep full coverage insurance on the vehicle you are purchasing.

"Mrs.   , this is a privacy notice, stating that you are protected from our dealership giving out your personal information to others.

"Mr._____, while Mrs. _____is signing the privacy notice, you can sign your portion of the title application right here. We are going to title this vehicle in both names in 'or' status so either one of you can sign the title without the other one present in the event you sell or trade the vehicle later."

See how the flow works?

Keep in mind that the paperwork in each dealership is slightly different. Adjust your word tracks depending on the requirements of your disclosure laws and your management guidelines.

The word tracks that I use are based on years of hearing the same questions over and over until I integrated my explanations. In time I developed a presentation that allowed me to complete my paperwork with little or no interruptions.

You can spend twenty minutes just signing this paperwork if you are not professional in this process.

Why not complete it in two or three minutes and have it out of the way?

I know you will get a contract reader once in a while, but don't let an exception rule the process.

7

BUILDING VALUE

Let's start our PRESENTATION.

Take out the menu that you prepared earlier. It would have been at the bottom of your paperwork stack, turned over so it looked like a blank page to your customer.

After you have completed signing all administrative paperwork, this and the visual aid tool for building value in your service contract should be the only two items left on your desk.

The visual aid for the service contract was designed to replace the brochure and other items I had been using as props to build value. We'll talk more about that later in the book.

Here is an example of the laminate.

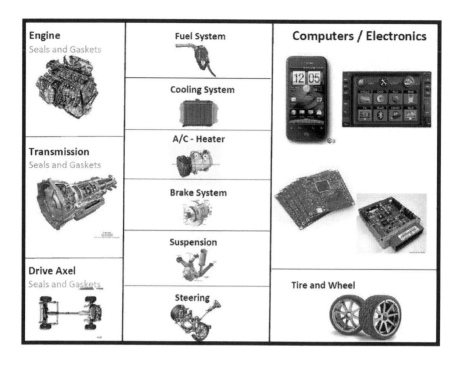

This tool has proven to be more valuable in selling service contracts than I could ever have imagined. Nearly every finance producer who has ever seen this has added it to their process, even if they didn't adapt this method of selling.

Slide the menu, with the blank side up, in front of you so you can begin writing on the back of it as you say,

FINANCE PERSON

"Mr. and Mrs. _____, we have all of the paperwork out of the way, I told you that wouldn't take long. I have a couple of things to go over with you that will only take TWO MINUTES." (NO PAUSE)

Do not underestimate the importance of the statement!

The reason I have named this process the

TWO MINUTE PRESENTATION

is because I believe this to be the most important statement I make during the presentation.

We talked a little earlier about the importance of having someone listen willingly. Positioning a customer to listen WILLINGLY will give us the best chance of getting them to see the value, and seeing the value is what will make them want to own the protection. Selling in F&I successfully is not about tricking someone into making a purchase they don't want to make. It's about showing them so much value (without overwhelming them) that they want to own it. Then it's just a matter of fitting it close enough to their budget that they can justify the purchase.

When I started in finance we only had three products available for sale—service contracts and life and A&H insurance (A & H is accident and health, or disability).

GAP didn't exist yet. There were rumors of theft protection products, but that was all. As time has passed, we now have nearly every kind of protection that can be imagined.

As you read I will refer to all other products as ancillary.

Life and A & H insurance is not sold as well in most dealerships as it could be. It is a very profitable product and should be treated with more value. When I first started trying to improve my sales dollars in finance, this is a product that I was overlooking. My general manager at the time asked me why I was not selling this product and I said the same thing that most finance people say,

"Most people are too old or they just aren't interested in this product."

That was not true. The truth was I didn't believe anyone wanted this product, so I didn't offer it.

From time to time, a customer would walk into my office and say, "I want insurance on my loan." When that happened I would always brag about how 'I' sold some insurance. The truth was, I took an order and filled it. There is a big difference between order taking and selling.

My general manager was a man who I have a great deal of respect for. He asked me if I would be willing to try an experiment with him and I agreed.

He challenged me to say to every finance customer who came into my office for the next thirty days,

"You don't want life or disability insurance, do you?"

Sounds kind of silly, doesn't it? Well, it's worse. He also wanted me to shake my head in a side to side fashion (as if to say no) while I asked.

Well, I promised that I would say it for 30 days and I did.

After a very short period of time I realized that people really would buy this product, and they did. Immediately my penetration for this product, which had been disgraceful, began to climb. By the time the thirty days was over, not only was I selling this product well, I was telling everyone I knew in the auto industry what an easy sell it was.

It became one of my key products. I used to start with these products, but because most dealerships no longer sell them I have moved the product to a different place later in the presentation.

Everyone sells GAP protection. I always start with GAP because the service contract   presentation is like the big main event for me. I use GAP to lead in with, make a huge production with my service contract and finish with a very light touch of my ancillaries.

Without pause, say,

"The first is GAP protection. Gap is easy to explain. Let's say, as an example, that you have a $20,000 loan and, sometime during the term of the loan, your vehicle becomes a total loss, either from collision or theft. Your insurance company will step in and write you a check, that's what you pay them to do."

"Unfortunately, you know as well as I do that, as soon as you drive off the lot and start putting miles on the vehicle, it begins to depreciate. Your insurance

company is going to write a check for current market value only, and if you happen to owe more than current market value, you could have a deficit. Gap is designed to step in and pay any 'GAP' that you would incur up to $50,000, plus it will pay your deductible up to $1,000. The second thing is warranty."

The exact coverage dollars and deductibles may vary, but you get the idea. Always round down when deciding on the amount for your example and use round numbers.

Draw an illustration of this on the blank side of your menu as you explain it.

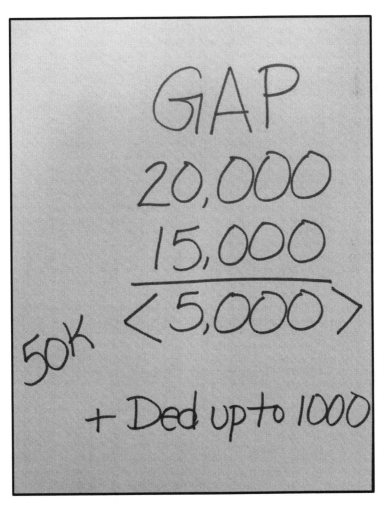

Without pause, say,

"The second thing is warranty," you'll notice that the last line in the GAP presentation already had this line. It's very important to make the transition from GAP to warranty without pause or you will create the question,

"How much is it?"

Once you've made the transition, continue with the warranty LEAD IN. I know you're already thinking,

Why is he not saying *"Extended service contract"*?

You would be correct, except I'm getting ready to explain the WARRANTY that they have now.

Use the word warranty when you can, if it meets compliance standards, because it's the only word that all customers understand every time.

As soon as we make the transition from what you have now to what you can add then, we start using the term 'extended service agreement' or whatever descriptive term you use to describe your product.

For the word track example that I'm going to use here I've picked a General Motors product. Adjust the word track appropriately for the product you're selling. If you are selling a used vehicle then describe the existing balance of the factory or whatever the dealership has included with the sale.

If there is no warranty at all, simply state that.

EXAMPLE:

"You have a 5 year / 100,000 mile powertrain warranty from the factory that is a great warranty, unfortunately it covers the power train only, which includes the engine, transmission and drive train only, and it may not cover

seals and gaskets 100% of the time. The good news is that you have a 3 year 36,000 mile limited bumper to bumper warranty that covers nearly everything and you can extend your 3 year 36,000 mile warranty out to 6 years / 100,000 mile coverage."

As I stated earlier, this is called a lead in.

As I start this explanation I should be writing this on the back of my menu, directly under the GAP explanation.

EXAMPLE:

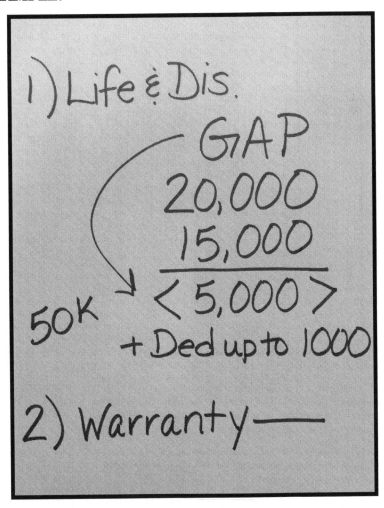

Only write down the highlights as you explain them through the word track on the last page.

Let me show you the coverage.

Now you introduce the visual aid to build value in your extended service contract.

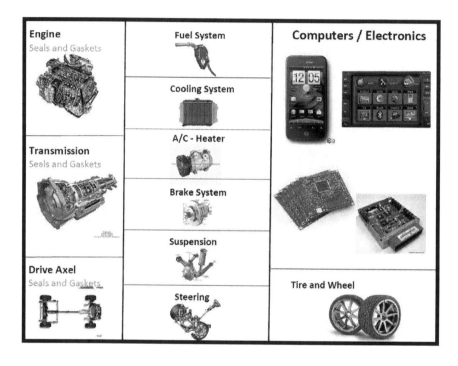

From left to right, begin this word track:

"Now your engine, transmission and drive axle are completely covered, including your seals and gaskets. You will also have protection for your fuel system, cooling system (which includes your radiator and water pump), your air conditioning and heating, brake system, your A.B.S., suspension and steering and, more important than anything, the computer and electronic system. It's generally not the transmission that's likely to fail; it's usually something like the computer chip that tells it to shift. So, whether you have a $3,000 computer failure, a $10,000 engine replacement or just

an oil leak in your driveway, you will be completely protected."

This visual aid has a tire and wheel component added at the bottom right hand corner. Your company may have a different product here. If that is the case, alter the visual aid. You may have theft protection, security system, or any number of different products that are available. You may even have a bundled product that includes tire and wheel, chip and ding, paint and fabric and key fob replacement. These are just a few examples.

Whatever the case, the visual aid is easily customized.

"Also your tires and wheels are completely covered for five years and unlimited miles."

If you have a bundled product you would change the description in the lower corner of the laminate to read Protection Package

And use this word track:

"Plus, you would have the protection package which will give you the full protection of your tires, wheels, door dings, glass chips, paint sealant, upholstery and key fob replacement for a full five years and unlimited miles."

Whatever your ancillary product(s) is, you will be far more effective if you only lightly mention the benefit here.

Later, when you present your menu, you can do a more involved value presentation if your customer questions the coverage.

Directly after you complete the word track we just covered, you end with,

"Now, I'll bet the big question you have is how much is all this going to cost me, isn't it?"

At this time you turn over your menu and begin in column one.

It's important to point out that, once you've completed the value building presentation that we just went over, do not re-sell it on the menu. When you turn that menu over, quickly review the products like this:

"In the first option you will have the service contract, GAP and the protection package (or tire and wheel etc.), and your new car payment including the added protection is only."

If you try to sell it again you will undo the value you have created.

I prefer the four term option with all the products in every column, because there is no choice except how long. Once they have objected or declined the added protection, we resort to the three step process for overcoming objections and closing.

For some, this is too aggressive. Build up to it with practice.

The revolution in this presentation is that all of this was presented in, including the four columns of options, one minute and fifty seconds.

(1 minute/50 seconds)

When you start with a pitch that takes less than two minutes, it gives you plenty of room to slow down to overcome objections and close when you don't get an immediate "YES."

By controlling the speed of your presentation, you will control the attention of your customer.

Most customers expect a very long, drawn out 'sell'. When your presentation begins to feel that way to them, they will react with bored or irritated body language.
Watch for it and speed up immediately.

Don't race through the presentation, but tailor your speed to their reaction and body language.

Don't increase your speed until you see it. If your customer continues to show interest at a slower pace, they are genuine

interested and probably need all the value you can build to make a decision.

Pay close attention. Selling is reading people. If you fail to read your customer(s) correctly, you could fail to sell them. If you are efficient with your paperwork and product presentation, you'll have plenty of time to close.

8

PRESENTING YOUR MENU

When you have completed your value building presentation, it's time to ask for the sale. You did the presentation on the back of your prepared menu for a reason.

So, without pause, turn your menu over and offer their option.

One thing that comes up often when I'm training one on one in a dealership is an objection at the end of the menu presentation.

The problem is confusion on the customer's part as to whether the payment you quoted them is in addition to the car payment or if it is the total price of the added protection.

Choose your wording carefully. Always say,

"Your NEW car payment is _____."

"With everything we just talked about, your new car payment for 36 months is only $889."

Anytime we fail to communicate our ideas efficiently and confuse our customers, we limit our success.

Always be very careful to avoid creating objections. We get enough when we do this correctly.

In this example of a four term menu that has every product in every column, I have chosen service contract, GAP, tire and wheel protection and key fob replacement.

Remember not to get caught up in the products. This presentation is about the philosophy of selling, we could insert any combination of products.

When you turn over your menu, always start with the top of the menu and disclose their monthly payment before any optional protection is added.

Producers who are afraid to do this are HOPING to sneak something past the customer. Great salespeople don't need to do that.

EXAMPLE:

"I'll bet the big question you have is, 'how much is all this going to cost', isn't it? Well, let me show you." (Turn over your menu)

"Your payment without any added protection is $$$$. Column one includes the VSC, GAP, tire and wheel protection and key fob replacement, if you decide to go with this one then your new car payment, for the short term of 36 months, will only be $$$$$, including all of the protection. At 48 months it will be $$$$, 60 months is $$$ and 72 is only $$$$. Which one works best for you?"

If you decide to use the other menu option, which has the shorter term for the first three columns and an extended term for the last column;

			RUSTAND, WHITNEY 2014 GMC TERRAIN

Repayment Options

Sale Price: $26,233.26 Sales Tax: $961.08 Rebate: $600.00 Trade Allowance: $6,000.00 Payoff: $4,930.73 Doc Fee: $499.50
License / Registration Fees and Taxes: $33.00

Preferred Plus	Preferred	Standard	Economy
CNA Vehicle Service Contract	**CNA Vehicle Service Contract**	**CNA Vehicle Service Contract**	**CNA Vehicle Service Contract**
· Pays 100% of covered Labor and Parts less deductible · Towing and Rental Allowance	· Pays 100% of covered Labor and Parts less deductible · Towing and Rental Allowance	· Pays 100% of covered Labor and Parts less deductible · Towing and Rental Allowance	· Pays 100% of covered Labor and Parts less deductible · Towing and Rental Allowance
Guaranteed Asset Protection	**Guaranteed Asset Protection**	**Guaranteed Asset Protection**	**Guaranteed Asset Protection**
· Picks up where the insurance company leaves off · In the event your vehicle is totaled or stolen and unrecovered, GAP pays the difference of your payoff and the insurance	· Picks up where the insurance company leaves off · In the event your vehicle is totaled or stolen and unrecovered, GAP pays the difference of your payoff and the insurance	· Picks up where the insurance company leaves off · In the event your vehicle is totaled or stolen and unrecovered, GAP pays the difference of your payoff and the insurance	· Picks up where the insurance company leaves off · In the event your vehicle is totaled or stolen and unrecovered, GAP pays the difference of your payoff and the insurance
Tire & Wheel	**Tire & Wheel**	**Tire & Wheel**	**Tire & Wheel**
· Protection from all road hazards · Repair or replace all tires and wheels	· Protection from all road hazards · Repair or replace all tires and wheels	· Protection from all road hazards · Repair or replace all tires and wheels	· Protection from all road hazards · Repair or replace all tires and wheels
Key Replacement	**Key Replacement**	**Key Replacement**	**Key Replacement**
· Replaces the key if lost, stolen, or destroyed.	· Replaces the key if lost, stolen, or destroyed.	· Replaces the key if lost, stolen, or destroyed.	· Replaces the key if lost, stolen, or destroyed.
Term: 36 Payment: $841.57	Term: 48 Payment: $639.27	Term: 60 Payment: $547.94	Term: 72 Payment: $437.10

I understand this is not a contract or offer to purchase. It is a description of the optional products that are available to purchase and the estimated monthly payment for each choice. I understand I must qualify to obtain financing and the payment may vary based on my credit. The base payment on 36 months is $767.48 on an interest rate of 2.59. The base payment on 48 months is $578.39 on an interest rate of 2.59. The base payment on 60 months is $466.19 on an interest rate of 2.59. The base payment on 72 months is $385.43 on an interest rate of 2.59. The finance charges, amount financed, total of payments, and total of payments including the down payment will be disclosed on my actual finance contract. The dealer makes no warranties, whether expressed or implied.

x_____   x_____   x_____
Purchaser's Signature   Co-purchaser's Signature   Date

Monday, March 03, 2014 5:57 PM

"If you decide to leave out the life insurance, your new payment is only $$$$."

"If you decide to leave the tire and wheel protection off, your new payment is only $$$$."

"With all the protection, by just extending the term a little, which you are already approved for, your new payment is only $$$$."

"Which payment works best for you?"

Remember the few things about the word track that are important:

- "Your new payment" helps keep your customer from saying, "Wait, I thought my payment was _____ ."

The statement "payment is only" is a subtle way of saying that the payment increase isn't that much.

- The 'menu sell' is great because it gives the customer choices, and none of the choices are "NO".

I conducted a study of several hundred customers to establish how many would buy the first time they were asked with this process and the results were very interesting.

Let's use 100 customers for this example and I'll round off the results to make this an easy example to explain. And even though I'm rounding off for the explanation, the results are accurate.

100

On average;

- Only 60 will purchase

- 1/3 of them (or 20) choose the lowest payment on the menu, regardless of how many products

- 1/3 make a choice and purchase after objection handling

- The last 1/3 only decide to purchase when the closer makes a good enough case to change their mind

It is very interesting to me that 1/3 of the buyers, when approached with this process; choose the lowest payment regardless of how many products are in the column.

This one fact should drive home the importance of changing the way we lay out our menu. Never offer a column at the end with only one or two products.

Regardless of how the menu is set up, the lowest payment on the menu should contain every product.

The second thing that is important is our closing skills and the method in which we use them. Closing skills will be the topic for the next chapter.

9

OVERCOMING OBJECTIONS

There are several ways to sell finance products. However, menu selling is the most widely used and the most effective.
When you give the options to your customer, it's very important to be quiet. The silence will create a sense of confrontation.
Some customers will buy to avoid confrontation.

If you serve the payment options to your customer and then start talking, your customer never has to face the feeling of confrontation and it becomes much easier to say, "No."

The 1/3 of the customers who are buyers will pick one of the options right away.

For the customer who says, "No," even after your powerful value building presentation, you need to become a closer.

If your customer says, "No," don't be afraid to say,

FINANCE PERSON

"I understand. Is it because you don't see any value in the added protection, or is it just price?"

You may get an answer like,

CUSTOMER

"Well, the payment is just too high."

This is a really good sign. If a customer's only objection is "too high," then they are not objecting to the product. If they see the value in the product, you have a chance to close them on at least a portion of the products on your menu.

The first attempt at closing this customer should always be,

"Well I understand. If that's the only problem, how much more money can you put down?"

It will surprise you how many people respond positively to this question. If a customer puts more money down, quote the new payment and assume they will say yes.

This is the most difficult step to convince finance producers to use consistently, because the results are only about 10% effective. I challenge you to consider the weight of this percentage. Ten percent is really amazingly good for a first attempt close.

If they still do not agree to buy after the first attempt, restructure your service contract and increase the deductible to reduce the cost of the service contract, which will lower your payment, and ask for the sale again.

(Remember, when we started the warranty value building presentation, we quoted a zero deductible. This was a set up to allow this closing technique. Also we should know, or can ask now, "How many miles do you drive per year?")

Explain:

"With a higher deductible, the premium cost is lower and that will make the payment less."

Lower the price of the service contract, adjust the gap a little, and maybe even your interest rate and ancillary if needed.
If you are this far along in closing and they haven't agreed to buy, you should know about where you will need to adjust your payment to close them.

If you don't get a close at this point, you have no choice but to start taking away product.

You will have decent product penetration simply by using this system, but for above average sales you will need to hold strong at these moments.

Explain to your customer:

"I know you see the value in the added protection, however, for us to fit this protection close enough to your budget, we will have to remove something. Of all of the added protection we've discussed, which one do you see the least value in?"

Our instinct tells us to remove the ancillary coverage, then the GAP and keep the service contract until the bitter end. The problem with this thinking is that it rarely works.

When we ask the customer,

"Which one do you see the least value in?"

The answer may be this:

"Well, I've had a service contract on my last three vehicles. The first two I never used and the last vehicle broke down and the plan didn't pay for the repair. I will never own another one as long as I live!"

Now, this may not happen, but if they did feel that way and had not voiced their concern, you would continue to sell something they wouldn't buy.

By asking them to choose, you're left with products that they will buy.

COMPLIMENT AND REDIRECT

Complimenting is a very important technique in leaving your customer feeling good about their decision.

Charge backs are a sad part of our industry, but they happen. Charge backs can be the result of a buyer's remorse.

If you handle your customer correctly in the final stages of the sale, however, you will dramatically reduce your percentage of charge backs

.

The radio and television industries use the term 'dead air'. Dead air is dangerous for finance people as well. When there is dead air, people change the station.

Once a customer says yes to buying, they need to feel good about their decision. Always compliment your customer after they say yes.

EXAMPLE:

"You've made a great decision."

Or

"I'm really glad that you decided to protect your investment."

Or

"I like the way you think."

You get the idea. Make them feel intelligent and they will be less apt to regret their decision later.

Also, if they do get buyer's remorse later, they will be less likely to come back to the dealership and cancel the product, especially if you have complimented them a lot and they like you. They won't want to disappoint you.

Once you have successfully reinforced their buying decision, re-direct.

Re-directing is a method of getting their mind off the buying decision and on to something else. This is effective when they buy, and also when you can't close them.

If you fail to get a sale, the next few moments can be very awkward. To relieve the tension in the air, re-direct.

EXAMPLE:

CUSTOMER

"No. I'm just REALLY not interested in buying anything!"

FINANCE PERSON

"No problem, I understand. So, where are you taking the new car for your first trip?"

CUSTOMER

"Well, we were thinking about going to _____."

FINANCE PERSON

"WOW! That sounds exciting."

Remember, people like to talk about themselves. Ask questions that will encourage that. The quicker you get off the subject of buying (or not buying) the quicker the customer will get comfortable, and the easier it will be to finalize the deal and get to the next one.

These examples will work on successful closes and failed ones.

10

THE TEN MOST FREQUENTLY ASKED QUESTIONS: FINALLY ANSWERED

How can people work effectively and timely in a finance office when there is a lack of professionalism from the sales staff regarding accurate paperwork?

Paperwork has always been, and will always be, the most frustrating problem that a Finance Manager faces administratively.

The problem is not that the salesperson is incapable; it's that they don't care. They don't look at this as an important part of their job. To them, it's just a necessary inconvenience.

I struggled with this problem for months when I first started doing F&I. Finally, I realized that I couldn't keep up with the volume of car deals unless something changed.

It occurred to me, that if I could get the salesperson to stay with me while I loaded the deal into the computer, at least I would have access to them when something was missing. Otherwise, I was always paging or trying to find them to get the missing information.

I went to my General Sales Manager and explained my problem. He was sympathetic and wanted a solution as much as I did.

Making customers wait too long is always bad for the dealership. It creates poor customer satisfaction, which creates poor retention.

He asked what I thought the solution was and I explained that I wasn't sure, but if he would give me the authority to ask the salesperson to sit down and stay with me until the entire deal was loaded, so as to ensure all of the information needed was in the deal jacket, or let me give the deal back to them and take the next deal in line.

We were generally busy enough that there was always another deal waiting.

We both knew that this would cause friction in the beginning, but we had to find a solution.

The first few times I said, "Have a seat while I load your deal," there was trouble. I would get responses like, "I'm too busy" or "I have to get the vehicle to cleanup" or, sometimes they would just say, "NO."

I didn't fight them at all. I simply laid their deal down and grabbed the next one in line. After they went over my head and found out that I had the support of the upper management, they started to sit down and let me do my job.
The funny thing is that the improvement in the quality of the paperwork was immediate.

Not only did they do a better job, now that they knew they would have to wait for me, I noticed as they were walking to my office, they would be looking through their deal jacket to make sure everything was there, and if it wasn't, they would turn around and go back until their deal was complete.

This is a solution that I used from then on and have helped hundreds of producers start using around the country. It seems too simple to work, but it does.

Why are salespeople so difficult to train on a proper T.O. to finance?

After I was in finance for about a year, I was invited to a class to train the sales staff to do a proper T.O. to finance.

I was excited because this is another age old problem. The salespeople do not like doing it as a rule, so they are no good at it. Once a salesperson has sold a vehicle, they perceive that their job is over. They want you, the F&I manager, to take over.

I agree with them. The more we can take off of the salesperson's plate, the more available they are to sell another vehicle. The class I attended was full of filler that had absolutely no usefulness in a real life situation, but I did take a few things away with me that were helpful.

The first thing was that I was paging the salesperson to bring the customer to me when I was ready. This is wrong on many levels, but the main problem is that the salesperson is not always with the customer when you are ready. So, you page them and then wait and wait and wait and sometimes wait some more.

When the F&I producer walks out to the salesperson's desk to get the customer, the process can continue even if the salesperson is not around.

If the salesperson is there and visiting with the customer, simply interrupt them, (politely) and introduce yourself. The problem with having the salesperson introduce you is they may stumble through the introduction and make everyone feel awkward and uncomfortable. When you control the introduction it will always be smooth.

In essence, remove the salesperson from the T.O. process completely and you will have solved the problem.

Why do some sales people refuse to set up the product sale with their customer prior to finance?

This problem is one of the easiest to explain. The salespeople don't like to do this because they are terrible at it.

Now, before we try and find a way to make them do it better, let's examine the process and decide whether they should do it at all. I was in my learning curve when this topic became important to me. I was beginning to pay attention to my customers' reaction to my presenting ability as I was improving my skills.

I started to notice that some customers had built a defense against purchasing any added protection, so I started to question them about any conversations with their salesperson prior to coming into my office.

What I started to realize is, that when a salesperson mentions an extended service contract and then leaves the customers alone, they naturally have a conversation between themselves about the protection. There is no advocate present to build value or to overcome objections, so if either ones decides "NO," then a defense is built that makes it almost impossible for the finance manager to overcome later on in the finance office.

When I realized this and started to train my salespeople to stop 'helping' me, they were relieved. Once again, they felt as though this wasn't their job and they were right.

Some finance people argue this point by giving examples of all of the customers that have bought these after being set up by the salesperson. These people would have bought anyway when the finance producer did a good presentation, so there is no downside. Interestingly, I found a study some years later that was done by Team One, (George Angus) that supports this position.

http://po.vresp.com/LurlBo

Why are customers always in a hurry when they get to finance?

Bad experiences. That's the only reason. There have been focus groups done by every manufacturer in the industry throughout the history of the automotive field. One of the most important things we've learned is that customers always feel like the process of signing takes too long.

The expectation of the process being too long creates the anxiety our customers feel, making them seem impatient.

The solution is to start the process by telling them how fast you will be taking care of their paperwork and what a great experience they are about to have.

I use this word track;

"Mr. and Mrs. Customer, when we get to my office don't get comfortable; I'm going to have you out of here so fast that your seat won't get warm. This is going to be the best experience you've ever had in a car dealership."

This will relieve the pressure and your customer will begin to relax. This selling method, (The Two Minute Presentation) will support the statement, reinforcing the fast and efficient process. It's up to us to change the experience for the customer.

Why do sales managers give hours (and sometimes days) to a salesperson to build value and close their product and yet they always rush the finance person?

The managers have had the same negative experience as the customer when it comes to the amount of time it takes to get deals in and out of the F&I office.

They do not want to get backed up in F&I, so they put pressure on the F&I producer, anticipating the problem.

Treat them like a customer. Tell them you will be ready in moments and then actually be ready. The system will increase your timeliness and build back their confidence levels over time.

Why do customers seem so defensive with finance people regarding their products?

Customers do not want to be sold. They want to be informed. The Two Minute selling system will give them the information they need to justify making the purchase.

Now your customer will buy from you instead of being sold by you.

Why is it so important to have a customer out of the finance office in a timely manner?

Retention is the number one reason for the customer to have a great experience. A timely experience in the finance office will help make that happen.

When customers have a great experience somewhere, they are more inclined to return. Returning to a place they feel good about gives you a better chance of selling them on their next visit. Always be conscious of the experience for the customer. Long term is what we are after. If you're in it for the short term you will never be successful.

Why can't the salespeople do a better job explaining rate to a customer?

Salespeople should never be put in the position to explain rate to a customer. That is the finance producers' job. When you send a salesperson out to talk rate with a customer you have decided to give up your income, or at least put it at risk.

The salespeople do not have the training or the credibility to close a customer on rate or products.

Don't risk your income. When rate or products come up prior to the customer being in the finance office, the F&I manager should always go out to the customer to handle the situation.

Why should I be charged back for a cancelation?

Charge backs are an unfortunate part of the industry, but we are all subject to them.

When a customer cancels a product or refinances a contract, the dealership has to pay back the prorated portion so the money the F&I manager was paid is no longer there and should be charged back appropriately.

Why do I have to focus on product sales instead of rate profit?

Rate is becoming less reliable in this industry. The government and the banks are getting more pressure than ever about protecting the customer against unfair practice by car dealers. Making a profit on rate is acceptable and the industry has done it since the beginning of finance offices in car dealerships.

The problem is a reputation of unfair practices toward customers has developed because some customers could be charged more than others in similar circumstances without justification.

Most professionals in the auto industry believe this unfair because the banks set the margin. No dealer can charge more than a bank will approve or their contracts would not fund.

It seems that right and wrong doesn't play into this as it should and the risk of losing our rate spread and going to flats exists. This makes profits on product sales more important than ever. For a dealership to survive in today's economy, product profits are a must.

11

THE TEN QUESTONS F&I MANAGERS
SHOULD BE ASKING

The problem with conventional F&I training is that the producer is being told to get better at selling the tough buyer.
We spend entirely too much time teaching people to sell the non-buyer.

Obviously, the more people we sell, the better our penetration of products becomes. In time, with training, practice and confidence we improve our skills. With improved skills come more sales. Increased profit comes from making more money on the customers we are already selling. The object of this book is to help increase profits and do it with a better customer experience.

We have talked about the selling technique of 'The Two Minute Presentation'; we've discussed the ten most commonly asked questions.

Now let's talk about the 'Ten Questions F&I Managers Should Be Asking'.

When we focus on what we should be asking we can begin to change the way we think.

Remember, "Nobody fails from setting goals too high and missing them, people fail from setting goals too low and hitting them."

How do I change my thinking?

Action!

Common opinion says, "If we change our thinking, our actions will begin to improve." I don't believe that.

I have come to believe that thinking will only change and stay changed when I take a chance and try a new action.

I have tried most new actions believing they wouldn't work. My success has been the result of taking the action anyway.

Changing my thinking happens when I take an action that I don't believe will work. Obviously, my thinking will only change from taking the action if the results are positive.

Try a new process and put everything you have into the effort, so the new action has a chance to work, and then let the results prove the new thinking.

It's easy for anyone to prove something won't work if they won't try it, or if they try it half-heartedly.

Try everything new with the most effort and sincerity you can and the results will prove themselves.

YOUR ACTION IS TO DO THE TWO MINUTE PRESENTATION!

How can I run good numbers with a bad desk?

Buying a vehicle and paying for a vehicle are two different events for the customer. We act like it is the same event and we're wrong. I say this because I train in stores every week that are afraid to let an F&I trainer have too much authority because they are afraid he will create problems for the sales managers and sales team.

I guarantee them that I can run my numbers in their environment without changing anything they are currently doing.

I can personally run 55% VSC, 65% GAP and 30% ancillary penetration in any well run dealership, regardless of the desking system and the sales people.

And I'll do it running over $1500 PRU. HOW?? It's easy. I use the 'Two Minute Presentation'.

If I worried about the ability of the desk managers or the sales people, I would limit my own success and I'm not willing to do that.

Blaming someone else is always a weak excuse.

Blaming someone else is always a weak excuse.

Blaming someone else is always a weak excuse.

Blaming someone else is always a weak excuse.

Blaming someone else is always a weak excuse.

Blaming someone else is always a weak excuse.

Blaming someone else is always a weak excuse.

Blaming someone else is always a weak excuse.

Do you think I said that enough times?

Build rapport, build value in your products, ask for the business, overcome objections and close EVERY TIME! Don't worry about what anyone else is doing.

Should the salespeople set up F&I?

Absolutely NOT!!

When a sales person mentions product in the F&I office to their customer prior to the T.O., they create the opportunity for the customers to discuss the value and build a defense against extra protection if they decide not to buy.

When this happens there is nobody there to change their mind.

71

By the time they get to the F&I office it is impossible to change their mind. Don't ask for help, EVER!

You will have more success and your sales people will do better because they don't want to do your job anyway. How do I improve my rapport building skills?

It starts with your sales person.

When the sales person brings the deal to you, interview them about the customer while you load the information into the computer.

Find out everything you can about them—what they like and don't like, what they do for fun. Do they have kids, grandkids or other family interests? Does he do something she doesn't like, or does she?

Find something to create situational humor. Remember, laughing is listening.

When you go out to the sales person's desk to get your customer, find out enough about that customer to immediately start a conversation about something important to them.

How can I improve my speed in F&I?

Do the same thing the same way, every time.

Anytime you change from a normal routine, you lose time and time is happiness to a customer. Time is also important to the sales person and the management team. Nobody wants to get backed up and make a customer wait. When a deal comes to F&I, write the time on the jacket.

When you have the deal loaded and leave your office to get the customer, write the time down on the jacket.

When you finish with the customer, write the time on the jacket. Find out where you are slow and concentrate on that first.

Be efficient, but don't let that keep you from overcoming objections and closing. It's okay to be fast as long as you don't miss sales by being in a hurry.

How do I build a better relationship with the salespeople?

That's easy. Treat them like they are customers instead of employees.

When I was moved into F&I from sales, the first thing I decided was to change the relationship between sales and F&I.

I was tired of being treated like an idiot by someone who was supposed to help me sell cars.

It has always puzzled me why finance managers don't understand the importance of a great relationship between them and sales.

The sales person is YOUR customer. They can cripple you if they want and you will never be able to prove it, if they're good.

They can also be your greatest ally if you partner with them to help you maximize your position with the customer.

Be consistent in your requirements of complete paperwork and readiness of the sales people, but be polite and remember that they have spent a lot of time and effort with their customer.

Respect them and help THEM sell a vehicle and they will become better at helping you succeed. Never talk down to them or become impatient with them if you can avoid it.

Remember that you need them too.

Work hard to get the tough car deals approved for your sales people too.

Never say, "This isn't a car deal." Nobody wants to hear that after they have invested time into a customer.

Submit everything and structure it to get a yes every time.

Regardless of what they tell you, submit it with the correct vehicle, enough cash down and the right term and payment to get a yes from the bank.

If the sales person or the manager cannot turn your yes into a car deal, at least they respect the fact that you were able to get them a way to go.

Be THE team member who changes the dynamic of your team.

How do I get more penetration of my products?

THAT'S SIMPLE.

Offer every product in every column, every time to every customer.

I have spent many years watching finance managers in every type of environment pick and choose who they offer certain products to.

A producer asked me once,

"When do you trust your gut feeling about what a customer will or won't buy?" The answer is simple,

"NEVER!"

I learned a long time ago never to decide for the customer. Let them decide. I just offer all of the products to all of the customers all of the time.

How do I improve my profit per deal?

The error came in the beginning. I was taught to work from cost up in finance. The managers would ask me questions like, "How much profit do you have on your service contract?" The correct answer should be, "As much as the bank will give me."

When the deal gets to me I determine the maximum advance I can get funded from the lender and fill that advance.

Some products are front add on products. Look at the advance available on the front and price your ancillary products accordingly.

GAP and Insurance coverages are generally set prices or have maximum retail prices. Set those prices and whatever is left over is what the service contract should be priced.

If you have a limited or capped call from the lender, put your lowest cost product in at the maximum price.

How many deals should I do in a month?

I did an average of 120 deals a month for nearly 6 years while I was developing this selling system.

I have come to believe that was too many.

The problem with most environments is they might do too few deals for two people or barely too many for one person.

In cases like this, pay plans can get skewed, customers can be forced to wait too long or the backup person could have less ability and cost the department profit.

Each environment has to be looked at on a case by case basis, but the correct number for a great finance person to maximize their profit is around 60 deals.

This gives plenty of time to do the entire job, which includes getting the paperwork done and in the office in a timely manner, getting the deal to the bank for funding, and a pay plan on that much volume should be set to challenge the producer to maximize profits and product penetrations.

What can I do to improve my skills in between training?

The most effective self-training tool that I used during my producing career was video recording.

I installed a camera in my office before it was popular. I never thought about compliance or liability; I just wanted to see what my customers were seeing. The value of the video review was priceless.

I also recommend YouTube. Watch everything you can watch on finance selling. You cannot expose yourself to anything that will harm you. Sort out the quality tips and throw out the rest. Read everything you can on human behavior and psychology. We are simply people dealing with people. And finally, teach as many people as you can. And teach them everything you know. When you help others, you will improve.

Learn and practice; then teach.

ABOUT THE AUTHOR

Michael is native to Arizona, where he grew up as a working cowboy on an old western style cattle ranch. By an early age he was working as a Farrier in the Phoenix area until an accident forced him into a less physically demanding occupation.

Sales seemed to be an acceptable alternative to the hard labor of ranching. He started in the auto industry in his early 20s as a salesperson at a Honda store in Prescott Arizona, after leaving an alarm company where he had started as a salesman and the last year had been working as a regional sales manager.

The alarm company had failed to provide the service that Michael was promising and he left the company with a one year non-compete agreement, which he honored.

The car sales job was originally meant to be temporary until the non-compete had been satisfied, but it was going so well by the end of the term and earning Michael more income than the management position at the alarm company had that it became the beginning of a new career path.

Michael sold for nearly five years before a finance position became available. The skills that he developed during this time helped him in the creation of "The Two Minute Presentation".

Michael spent six years as a finance manager and director before a promotion to sales manager. From there he was promoted to General sales manager for a few years and then made a very unusual transition into the office as the comptroller.

When offered that position, he asked, "Why would you want me to work in the office instead of a production position?" The owner of the dealership said, "I can teach you accounting but I can't teach someone to be honest."

The position paid the same as the General Manager position and offered a great learning experience, so Michael took the job and after a few years was promoted to General Manager and CFO of the company, which was a five rooftop group selling over six hundred units per month when he left.

Michael was recruited and relocated to Alabama by another large auto group and has made Alabama his home. He lives south of Mobile on Mon Louis Island with his wife Shelly. They have four grown children, three surviving and one they lost, Augustus, at the young age of twenty one, through a very sad accident.

They have eight grandchildren and are very involved with their children's lives.

For fun, Michael and Shelly like to travel. They spent years riding horses and motorcycles, boating and golfing.

Michael has such a vast working knowledge of a car dealership that he is able to understand the importance of doing a good job in F&I. not only for the added income, but also for CSI. Customer retention has become so important in the industry today.

The "Two Minute Presentation" was designed over nearly ten thousand car deals and is proven to give the customer the best experience they've ever had buying a vehicle.

Michael has trained hundreds of finance people in his career and is quickly becoming one of the most well recognized names in the industry.

The success stories are truly unbelievable.

With this system, producers sell more products, make more profit and do it easier and faster than anyone believed was possible.

In 2008 Michael started his training company and has enjoyed great success. Michael partnered with a large product provider company in 2011 and manages the training portion of the company, Paragon Dealer Training, as the Director of Training and Dealer Income Development.

Paragon Dealer Training has the Endorsement of several large service contract and product companies and has developed all of their training online at Paragon Digital Training.

Michael is current, innovative and creative. He has stayed ahead of the technical growth of the industry.

43206470R00050

Made in the USA
Lexington, KY
26 June 2019